ULURU

Australia's Aboriginal Heart

BY **CAROLINE ARNOLD**   PHOTOGRAPHS BY **ARTHUR ARNOLD**

CLARION BOOKS / NEW YORK

Clarion Books
a Houghton Mifflin Company imprint
215 Park Avenue South, New York, NY 10003
Text copyright © 2003 by Caroline Arnold
Photographs copyright © 2003 by Arthur Arnold

Additional photo credits: Australian Tourist Commission, p. 42; Caroline Arnold, pp. 6, 39 (left), 44 (bottom), 46, 47 (bottom), 60, 61.

The text was set in 13-point Cicero.

www.houghtonmifflinbooks.com

Printed in China.

Library of Congress Cataloging-in-Publication Data
Arnold, Caroline.
Uluru, Australia's Aboriginal heart / by Caroline Arnold ; photographs by Arthur Arnold.
p. cm.
Summary: Describes Uluru, formerly known as Ayers Rock, in Australia's Uluru-Kata Tjuta National Park, its plant and animal life, and the country's Aboriginal people for whom the site is sacred.
ISBN 0-618-18181-4 (alk. paper)
1. Uluru-Kata Tjuta National Park (N.T.). 2. Australian aborigines—Australia—Northern Territory—Antiquities—Juvenile literature. 3. Australian aborigines—Australia—Northern Territory—Religion—Juvenile literature. 4. Sacred space—Australia—Northern Territory—Juvenile literature. 5. Dreamtime (Australian aboriginal mythology)—Australia—Northern Territory—Juvenile literature. [1. Uluru-Kata Tjuta National Park (N.T.). 2. Australian aborigines.] 1. Arnold, Arthur, ill. II. Title.
GN667.N67 A76 2003
994.01—dc21   2002015542

SCP 10 9 8 7 6 5 4 3 2 1

TITLE PAGE: *View of Uluru from the Liru walk, with wattle bush (tjuntala) in bloom.*

PAGES 2-3: *Desert oaks (kurkara) and spinifex grass (tjanpi) on the sand plain west of Uluru.*

Contents

A Giant Red Rock

In the middle of the Australian continent, a huge sandstone rock more than a thousand feet high rises from the flat desert floor. It is the world's biggest single rock and one of Australia's most impressive natural wonders. For at least ten thousand years, the land around this imposing landmark has been inhabited by Aboriginal, or native, people called the Anangu. Their name for the giant red rock is Uluru. Uluru plays a central role in the traditional beliefs of the Anangu and is a sacred site associated with stories about the creation of the land and all living things on it.

Uluru is also one of Australia's most popular tourist destinations. Each year nearly half a million people from all over the world visit it and the nearby large rock formation of Kata Tjuta. A close look at these amazing rocks and the surrounding arid landscape helps us to learn not only about the relationship between Australia's Aboriginal people and their environment but also about the continent's vast interior regions and how plants, animals, and people have adapted to the harsh desert climate.

Uluru.

5

Uluru and Kata Tjuta are located in Australia's Northern Territory, 467 kilometers (290 miles) southwest of the town of Alice Springs. For many years Uluru has been known to most people as Ayers Rock, the name given to it in 1873 by explorer William Christy Gosse, who was the first European to climb to the top. He named the giant monolith in honor of Sir Henry Ayers, the chief secretary of South Australia at the time. The first European to see Kata Tjuta was another explorer, Ernest Giles. He saw the rocky outcrop in 1872 and named it Mount Olga in honor of the queen of Spain. The formation became known as the Olgas.

The central Australian desert, with Kata Tjuta in the distance.

Uluru and Kata Tjuta are within a large area called the Petermann Aboriginal Reserve, which was set aside in 1920 by the Australian government as a place where Aboriginal people could live away from the developing towns and grazing lands to the east. It was similar in many ways to the reservations where Native Americans live in the United States. In 1958, the Australian government removed Uluru, Kata Tjuta, and the land around them from the reserve and established the area as a national park and wildlife preserve. Although the new national park made it possible for more visitors to come to Uluru and Kata Tjuta, it created problems for the Anangu, disrupting their lives and often disturbing their sacred sites.

Uluru and Kata Tjuta are located close to Australia's geographic center.

In 1976, the Northern Territory government passed the Aboriginal Land Rights Act, which allowed Aboriginal people to claim rights to land where they had traditionally lived, as long as it was outside town boundaries and no one else owned or leased it. Three years later, the Anangu began the process of claiming Aboriginal ownership of Uluru and Kata Tjuta. On October 26, 1985, in recognition of the Anangu's long-standing occupation of the area and its significance to Anangu culture, the Australian government returned ownership to them. The Aboriginal people now lease

Vegetation around Uluru consists mainly of grasses, shrubs, and a few scattered trees.

Welcome to Aboriginal Land

Uluṟu-Kata Tjuṯa National Park

Pukul ngalya yanama
Ananguku ngurakutu

Pukulpa pitjama
Ananguku ngurakutu

World Heritage Area

the land back to the government as Uluṟu-Kata Tjuṯa National Park and manage it jointly with the Australian Nature Conservation Agency. They also control public access to their sacred sites and other important cultural areas within the park. Tourist facilities, once located at the base of the rock, have now been moved outside the park boundaries to the small community of Yulara.

The total area of the Uluṟu-Kata Tjuṯa National Park

Uluṟu-Kata Tjuṯa National Park was placed on the World Heritage list in 1987.

is 1323 square kilometers (511 square miles.) It is protected as a United Nations World Heritage Site both for its cultural and historical value and for its unique natural history. Within the park are many plants typical of the central Australian desert, among them a number of rare species. There is also a wide variety of animal life, including more kinds of reptiles than exist in any similar area of Australia.

Australia's First People

Aboriginal people are Australia's original inhabitants, and according to traditional beliefs, they have lived there since the beginning of time. (The English word "aboriginal" comes from Latin roots meaning "from the very first.") Archaeological evidence suggests that the first humans arrived in Australia about forty thousand years ago, or possibly somewhat earlier, crossing the sea from southeast Asia and landing in northwest Australia and New Guinea. People then spread out over the continent, developed different languages, and adapted to the particular resources of the places where they lived. For centuries they lived a semi-nomadic life, hunting and gathering food and using tools made of stone, bone, shell, and wood.

According to the 1996 census, about 350,000 people in Australia identify themselves as Aboriginal or of indigenous origin. Most of these people live in northern and central Australia, some in towns and cities, but many others in more remote places.

The northwest side of Uluṟu.

The history of Aboriginal people in Australia since the arrival of European settlers a little more than two centuries ago has been one of conflict. Many aspects of Aboriginal culture have been lost as people have been forced to give up their traditional life. For instance, while there were once 250 separate Aboriginal languages, only thirty are spoken today. Yet many traditions survive, and in recent years there have been increased efforts to keep these Aboriginal cultural practices alive.

All Aboriginal people belong to small groups called clans. Clans are linked by common religious traditions, intermarriage, overlapping territories, and shared dialects. The dialects spoken by most of the Aboriginal people who inhabit the area around Uluru are Pitjantjatjara and Yankunytjatjara. These are dialects of the Western Desert language of the region, the largest language group of Aboriginal Australia, with about four thousand speakers. All of the people who live at Uluru, including those who speak other Western Desert dialects, refer to themselves as the Anangu, which is a Pitjantjatjara word meaning Aboriginal. Most of the Aboriginal words used in this book are from the Pitjantjatjara. They are noted in italics except for proper names. The underlining of letters in certain words, like Uluru, is part of the Pitjantjatjara spelling system.

Aboriginal people in Australia identify themselves with one or more ancestral animals or other beings.

The rufous hare wallaby (mala) was once common throughout the desert regions of Australia but is now extinct there. It can still be found on two small islands off the coast of Western Australia, and a few are being reintroduced on the mainland. Although this rabbit-sized marsupial may dig a short burrow, it often takes shelter under large clumps of grass.

According to tradition, each person is descended from one of these spirits and possesses some of its life force. Many ancestral beings were based on people, or on animals such as snakes or birds, but they often were of a giant size or had unusual powers. Others were supernatural. The ancestors that many of the Anangu associate with are the Mala, or rufous hare wallaby, people. The hare wallaby is a small relative of the kangaroo. Places where the Mala people camped, prepared food, and met for ceremonies at Uluru are important sites for the Anangu today.

Tjukurpa

The Aboriginal way of viewing the world is through their tradition of Tjukurpa and its emphasis on spiritual understanding and detailed knowledge of the land and its resources. The word "Tjukurpa" has several meanings. First, it is the creation time, when ancestral beings moved across the empty land and gave it shape. As these beings roamed the world, they camped, hunted, made fires, dug for water, fought each other, and performed ceremonies. In the process the land was marked with a record of their activities. For instance, according to tradition, some of the huge holes in the side of Uluru are spear marks from an ancestral hunt, and some of the boulders are giant eggs or chunks of meat. The national park is criss-crossed by a network of tracks that mark ancestral journeys connecting Uluru and Kata Tjuta as well as other sites within and outside the park.

All geographic features of the Earth as well as all its plants and animals are the result of activities in the

Sunrise in the desert.

creation time. The spirits of the ancestral beings remain in the land today and can be seen in rocks, trees, animals, and all aspects of the physical and natural world. Their power is especially strong in places where there were significant events in the creation time. As Aboriginal people go about their daily lives in the natural world, they are in constant contact with the ancestral spirits.

Tjukurpa is also the traditional law that guides daily life. It provides the rules for behavior and for living together. It determines when ceremonies will take place and who may participate in them, the proper relationships between men and women—for instance, whom a person may marry—and even what to eat and how to prepare food. Knowledge about animals and

The emu (kaḻaya) is a large flightless bird that is seen occasionally at Uluṟu. Knowledge of the emu and its role in the natural world—like that of all living things—is part of Tjukurpa.

plants and caring for the land that supports people's existence are also part of Tjukurpa.

Tjukurpa is the foundation of Aboriginal culture and joins the Aboriginal people to the natural and physical world. It explains the origin of these relationships, their meaning, and how they must be maintained. The various aspects of Tjukurpa are passed from one generation to the next in story, song, dance, art, and ceremony. People learn about Tjukurpa in stages throughout life, progressing through a series of steps to higher degrees of specialized knowledge. In a display in the cultural center at Uluṟu-Kata Tjuṯa National Park, the Aṉangu say this about Tjukurpa: "This Law was given to us by our grandfathers and grandmothers, our fathers and mothers, to hold in our heads and in our hearts."

A Sacred Place

Ulu<u>r</u>u has special significance for all Aboriginal people because of its important role in sacred ceremonies and in stories of ancestral beings in the creation time. As you walk along the base of the rock, you can see landmarks connected with some of these stories. Many other stories connected with Uluru are kept secret and are known only by the A<u>n</u>angu. According to Aboriginal law, just a few of Ulu<u>r</u>u's stories can be told to outsiders—and then only by designated storytellers. Even among the Aboriginals, certain stories, or details from them, are restricted to those who have been properly initiated or selected.

Here are a few of the ancestral beings whose stories are connected to features you can see at Uluru. When you visit the park, you can find out more about these sites from park rangers, tour guides, brochures, and signs posted along the trail.

The Mu<u>t</u>itjulu water hole.

Linear marks high on the rock at Muṯitjulu are signs of the snakes Kuniya and Liru.

KUNIYA THE PYTHON

In the creation time, Kuniya the python battled Liru, a poisonous snake, in an area on the southeast side of Uluṟu known as Muṯitjulu. Kuniya is the ancestor of the woma python, a large snake found in the sand plains around Uluṟu. Liru is the ancestor of all poisonous snakes. You can see a variety of features at Muṯitjulu that are associated with the story of Kuniya and Liru. Since ancient times this area near the Muṯitjulu water hole has been a traditional camping site for the Anangu.

THE MARSUPIAL MOLE

Marsupial moles are small animals that live in burrows in the dunes and sand plains around Uluru. Although they spend most of their time tunneling through the ground searching for food, they occasionally come up to the surface. In the creation time there was a giant marsupial mole named Itjaritjari. On the west side of Uluru you can see the cave where Itjaritjari lived.

23

WILLY WAGTAIL WOMAN

The willy wagtail is a small black-and-white bird that can be found throughout Australia. It hops about, wagging its tail and singing a cheerful song that sounds much like its Anangu name, *tjintir-tjintirpa*. In the creation time, a willy wagtail woman lived at Uluru in a cave called Ikari. Her cave, which is on the southeast side of Uluru, has the shape of a smile.

Ikari, the cave of the Willy Wagtail Woman.

Lichen is a plant consisting of algae and fungus growing in close association. The large patch of lichen on Uluṟu is part of the story of the Blue-tongued Lizard Man. It represents smoke from a fire.

THE BLUE-TONGUED LIZARD MAN

The blue-tongued lizard is a fat, medium-sized lizard found across much of Australia. Its ancestor is Lungkaṯa. The crested bellbird is a small bird that lives in Australia's dry inland regions. Its ancestor is Panpanpalala. In the creation time, an argument over an emu between Lungkaṯa and two Panpanpalala brothers took place on the south side of Uluṟu.

The Geology of Uluṟu and Kata Tjuṯa

The scientific explanation of the rock formations in central Australia goes back to events that occurred about 550 million years ago, during what geologists call the Cambrian period. At that time, movements in the Earth's crust created a huge mountain range south and west of Uluṟu and Kata Tjuṯa. Over the next 50 million years these mountains eroded, forming a broad plain consisting of layers of sediment at least 2.5 kilometers (1.5 miles) thick. Then, between 340 and 310 million years ago, the Earth's crust shifted dramatically, lifting the land surface and tilting the layers of sediment upright. Today you can see those layers as almost vertical ridges on the sides of Uluṟu.

The layers of sediment that form Uluṟu are tipped almost ninety degrees from horizontal. The outer surface of Uluṟu is a flaky "skin" created by the chemical decay of the minerals in the rocks.

ULURU

Uluru rises 340 meters (1115 feet) above the surrounding desert and at its highest point is 862.5 meters (2829 feet) above sea level. The distance around the base is about 9.4 kilometers (5.8 miles.) Weathering by wind and water over the last 300 million years has given Uluru its present shape. As tiny bits of rock wore from the surface and washed away, they spread out to form the broad plain surrounding the rock. What we see of Uluru is only the top of a

Caves at the base of Uluru may be the result of ground-level moisture, which causes the rock to erode.

Large birds, like the black-breasted buzzard (kirkinpa), soar on updrafts over Uluru.

much larger rock. Scientists estimate that Uluru may extend underground as far as 5.8 kilometers (3.6 miles.)

Uluru is composed of a coarse-grained rock called arkose. Arkose is a mixture of small particles of sand, quartz, and feldspar, along with traces of iron oxides, clay, and small pieces of other rocks. When iron in the arkose is exposed to oxygen during the weathering process, it turns a rusty red. This gives Uluru its distinctive hue. Inside Uluru's caves, where the iron has not been oxidized, the arkose is gray.

Shallow caves along the edge of the rock just above ground level are distinctive features of Uluru. Traditionally, these caves provided the Anangu shelter from the sun and rain, and were places for sacred ceremonies and for rock paintings. Honeycomb-shaped caves high on the rock are homes for small animals and nesting birds.

In the cave of Ikari on Uluru's southeast side, there are animal bones and teeth that have accumulated over hundreds of years and been preserved in the dry desert climate. Some of the bones are from animals that died there, while others were brought by predators, such as owls and dingoes. About forty species of mammals are represented, revealing the diversity of life around Uluru. The bones also provide proof that animals such as the bilby (*ninu*) and rufous hare wallaby, species that are now extinct at Uluru, once lived there.

KATA TJUTA

Kata Tjuta is located about 33 kilometers (20 miles) west of Uluru. Although it was formed by the same geologic forces that shaped Uluru, it is composed of a coarser conglomerate rock—a gravel consisting of pebbles, cobbles, and boulders, which has been cemented together by sand and mud. Most of the gravel pieces are granite or basalt. Like Uluru, the rock of Kata Tjuta contains iron that has oxidized on the surface, giving it a red hue. The sediment layers of Kata Tjuta are tipped only slightly from the horizontal plane, about fifteen degrees.

Kata Tjuṯa at sunset.

Instead of being a single large rock like Uluṟu, Kata Tjuṯa has cracked and broken to form thirty-six separate domes and a network of valleys and canyons. The highest dome of Kata Tjuṯa is 546 meters (1790 feet) above the ground. It is the highest point in the park.

From a distance, the rounded domes of Kata Tjuṯa look like the tops of giant spheres. Kata Tjuṯa, which means "many heads," is closely connected to Aṉangu culture and Tjukurpa. Because of its deep spiritual significance, its stories are not permitted to be told to non-Aboriginals. Public access to the area is limited.

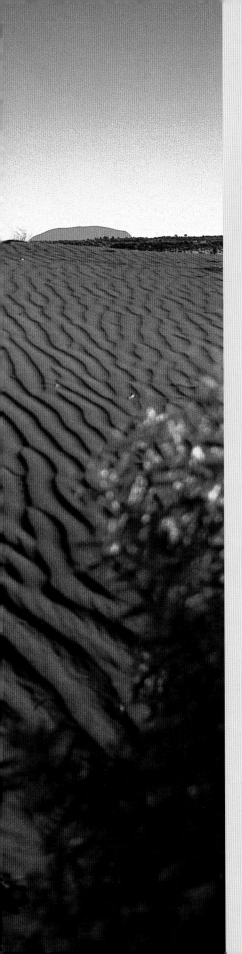

A Desert Landscape

Much of the interior of Australia is a vast desert, ranging from extremely dry to semiarid regions. Uluru-Kata Tjuta National Park is in a semiarid zone that includes four distinct habitats, each supporting a different type of plant and animal life.

The most common habitats in the park are the sand plains, called *pila*, along with the sand dunes, called *tali*. They are usually covered with spinifex grass (*tjanpi*) and scattered trees, such as the desert oak (*kurkara*), a type of casuarina tree.

Spinifex is a tough plant, and because of its prickly tips is sometimes also called porcupine grass. It grows in round clumps and has a deep root system that holds on to the desert sand and helps prevent erosion. It can survive all but the worst droughts. Few animals can eat the dry spinifex, but it is important in providing shelter for mice, lizards, and other small animals. The Anangu

Although most sand dunes around Uluru are covered with vegetation, some are blown bare by the wind. Iron oxide makes the sand red.

gather a sticky resin from one type of spinifex to make a glue called *ki̱ti̱,* which is used in making and repairing stone and wood tools.

In the crevices and canyons of Uluṟu and Kata Tju̱ta are rocky outcrops the A̱nangu call *puḻi.* Only plants with shallow root systems can grow there. Water that collects in pools in *puḻi* attracts birds and animals. During extended periods of drought, *puḻi* are places where water is most likely to be found and where wildlife and food plants can continue to survive. For the A̱nangu who lived at Uluṟu in the past and for the early European explorers in the Australian desert, *puḻi* were always welcome oases.

Bloodwood trees (muur-muurpa) rely on water that sinks into the soil at the base of Uluṟu. They get their name from their thick red sap.

The flat, open woodlands at the base of Uluṟu and Kata Tju_ta are called *puti* by the Anangu. *Puti* are where the Anangu find many of their foods and building materials. Because of the variety of plants that grow in *puti*, many animals go there to feed, and birds nest in the trees. Trees and shrubs that are found in *puti* include mulga trees (*wanari*), a type of acacia; bloodwood trees (*muur-muurpa*), a kind of eucalyptus; and a shrub called the witchetty bush (*ilykuwara*). A plump white grub known as *maku* lives in the roots of the witchetty bush and is a favorite food of the Anangu.

The most common tree in Australia's arid and semiarid regions is the mulga. Groves of mulga grow at the base of Uluṟu, and mulga shrub lands are found throughout the park. Mulga leaves, which are actually flattened leafstalks called phyllodes, help funnel rainwater down the branches and trunk of the tree to the soil, maximizing the amount of moisture available to the tree's roots.

Every part of the mulga tree is useful to the Anangu.

Mulga trees (wanari) and spinifex (tjanpi).

They cut down the trunks and heavy branches to make spear throwers and use the smaller branches for barbs, spearheads, boomerangs, digging sticks, and firewood. They construct shelters and windbreaks with small, leafy branches. The Anangu also collect and grind mulga seeds into an edible paste. Another food from the mulga is a sticky gum, which the tree produces as a defense against attacks by insects. Anangu children eat the sweet gum like candy.

The Seasons

Because Australia is in the southern hemisphere, its cycle of seasons is opposite those north of the equator. The coldest time of year is in June and July, and the hottest is in December and January. At Uluru, temperatures can go below freezing in winter and well above 38 degrees Celsius (100 degrees Fahrenheit) in summer. The windiest time of year is from August to November. Wind speeds are usually about 1 to 2 kilometers (.6 to 1.2 miles) an hour, but occasionally winds of up to 90 kilometers (56 miles) an hour have been recorded. For people like the Anangu, whose survival has traditionally depended on the land, a knowledge of the weather and its effect on food resources is essential.

Zebra finches (nyii-nyii) are small seed-eating birds that are common at Uluru and usually seen in large flocks.

Rattlepod grevillea grows in tall, open shrub lands and blooms in August and September.

Parrot peas (paltu-paltupa) grow on sand hills in August and September. The leaves can be mashed and used to treat snake bites.

The military dragon (tjantjalka) is a small lizard that can be seen in warm weather among the spinifex. When chasing insects, it runs on its hind legs.

The Anangu divide the year into seasons, which they recognize by temperature and rainfall and by the life cycles and activities of plants and animals. A warm steady wind typically blows from the north-west in August and September, and this is the season when animals breed, flowers bloom and produce fruit, and hibernating reptiles emerge from their hiding places. The weather gradually grows hotter during the next few months, and by December storm clouds begin to gather. January through March is the rainy season, and many food plants flower at this time. By the end of April the weather becomes cool again and reptiles go into hibernation. May, June, and July are the cold months. Then the earth gradually warms, and the cycle of growth begins once again.

Water

Water is a precious resource in the desert. Rainfall is erratic in the Australian interior, and droughts can last several years. The average yearly rainfall at Uluru is less than 23 centimeters (9 inches) and most of this occurs in late summer. There is little permanent water in the area around Uluru because the sandy soil soaks up even the heaviest downpours. Seasonal streams and pools dry up quickly.

The base of Uluru is one of the few places where water can usually be found year round. When it does rain, water cascades down the sides of the rock and collects in pools. Mutitjulu, on the south side of the rock, is the most reliable water hole at Uluru and a natural game trap. Animals go there to drink, and traditionally this is where the Anangu can easily find game to hunt. Kantju Gorge, on the northwest side of Uluru, has another large semi-permanent water hole. The steep canyon walls make this shady spot cool and peaceful even on the hottest days. The Anangu ask that visitors walk silently and respectfully when they come to Kantju Gorge because of its closeness to several sites that have great spiritual significance.

Knowledge of where to find water has been passed down through many generations of Anangu. Scattered across the desert are a few permanent water holes where underground water comes to the surface. During the rainy season there are also temporary water

Muṯitjulu water hole.
The spearwood bush
(urtjanpa) grows
among the boulders
of Muṯitjulu.

holes that fill up in depressions of the plain in places where clay in the soil prevents water from draining. Water can also be found by digging. River red gums, a species of eucalyptus that grows along dry river beds, have long water-seeking taproots and are a good indication that there is moisture below the surface. The Anangu know how to find water that has collected in the hollows of trees and also how to get moisture from certain kinds of tree roots.

Desert Wildlife

Although the vast desert regions of Australia's interior would seem to be an inhospitable environment, a surprising variety of plants and animals live and thrive there. Uluru and Kata Tjuta are magnets for wildlife because they have a reliable water supply and the rich vegetation that grows around their bases provides food and shelter. You can find a wide range of wildlife in the national park, each species having its own special adaptations to the dry desert climate.

More than twenty native mammals can be found at Uluru, including large marsupials like the red kangaroo (*malu*) and wallaroo (*kanyala*), and many smaller species like the marsupial mole (*itjaritjari*) and the spinifex hopping mouse (*tarkawara*). The echidna (*tjilkamata*), also called a spiny anteater, is found among the boulders of Uluru and in burrows in the ground. It is one of two species of monotremes, or egg-laying mammals, that live in Australia. The caves

Red kangaroos (malu) can survive with little water, getting most of the moisture they need in their food.

and crevices of Ulu̱ru are home to several kinds of small bats (pa̱tupiri). You can see them when they come out at dusk to catch insects. Often you can hear the barking of dingoes (papa) at night. Dingoes are wild dogs that came to Australia from southeast Asia about 3500–4000 years ago. In the past, the A̱nangu sometimes raised dingo pups as hunting dogs.

Dingoes (papa) are found throughout Australia, except in Tasmania.

Sharp spines protect echidnas (tjilkama̱ta) from most predators. Their diet consists mainly of ants and termites.

Birds are the most noticeable wildlife in the park. They can be seen soaring high over the tops of the rocks, perching in trees and bushes, and searching for seeds and insects on the ground. At least 178 species are found within the park, ranging from flocks of noisy galahs (*piyar-piyarpa*) to graceful falcons (*kirkinpa*) and powerful wedgetail eagles (*walawuru*). The Anangu name birds by their calls. If you listen to the repetitive chirp of the zebra finch, "nyii-nyii," or the soft twittering of the crested pigeon, "aralapalpalpa," you can hear how those sounds became the birds' Anangu names.

Galahs (piyar-piyarpa) are common at Uluru.

Although some birds come to Uluru only after periods of rain, others live there year-round. Like other animals, birds need to drink, and most live in places where they are within flying distance of water. Birds that eat insects or animals can get some needed

The carpet python (kuniya), which can grow up to six feet long, is found in rocky areas of the central Australian desert.

moisture from this food. In order to reduce water loss from evaporation during extremely hot weather, desert birds reduce their activities and stay in the shade.

The seventy-two species of reptiles in the park include many snakes and a variety of lizards. The fat goanna lizard is a favorite food of the A̲nangu, who catch it on the ground or in trees and then cook it on hot coals. The largest lizard of central Australia is the perentie (*ngi̲ntaka*), which can grow to be nearly 2.5 meters (8 feet) long. Perenties live in burrows in the sides of hills.

A few amphibians also live in the park. In cool weather several kinds of frogs and toads (*nga̲nngi*) can

Ants are the primary food of the thorny devil lizard (ngiyari).

Tracks in the sand reveal the nighttime activities of several animals.

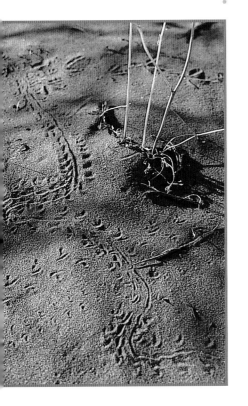

be found near water holes. In hot weather they go underground.

Ants, termites, grasshoppers, crickets, moths, and beetles are among the wide variety of insects found around Uluru. They multiply rapidly after periods of heavy rain and provide food for lizards, snakes, birds, and other animals.

Like desert animals everywhere, those of Australia's central regions have adapted to the arid climate. Much of the animal activity takes place at night, when the air is cooler and daytime predators are asleep. In the morning, tracks in the sand reveal who passed that way during the night. Daytime winds then smooth over the sand, making a clean slate to record the next night's activities. The Anangu are experts at identifying and following tracks through the desert.

THE CHANGING LANDSCAPE

A number of animals that formerly lived at Uluṟu, including the rufous hare wallaby, burrowing bettong, bilby, and common brushtail possum (*wayuta*), are now extinct in the park. The disturbance by visitors and the destruction of the animals' natural habitat are two of the main reasons they have disappeared. As elsewhere in Australia, native animals have also become endangered because of the intrusion of non-native species that killed them, ate their food, or took over their territories. Many of these imported ani-

Camels can travel up to thirty miles a day as they move across the Australian desert.

mals, including cats, dogs, red foxes, and rabbits, were brought by European settlers, who first came to Australia in 1788.

Few outsiders settled in central Australia before the completion of the telegraph line joining Adelaide and Darwin in 1872. Since then, the population has grown steadily. Alice Springs, the largest town in the region, now has more than 25,000 people. During the early years of European settlement, the only reliable mode of transportation in the desert was by camels, which were imported from Asia. After roads and railway lines were built, camels were no longer needed, and in the 1920s many were let loose to fend for themselves. Camels are well suited to the Australian outback. They can go for days without food or water and will eat almost any plant food, including thorny scrub, dry twigs and leaves, and seeds. Today Australia has the largest wild camel population in the world, with an estimated 200,000 animals. You can often see camels roaming the desert near Uluṟu. However, camels endanger native wildlife by destroying their habitat.

The landscape of the desert has also been changed by the introduction of non-native plants such as buffel grass and rubydock. Park managers are working to rid the park of non-native plants wherever they threaten native species. In the future, they may also reintroduce some animals, such as the brushtail possum, that once made their homes at Uluṟu and Kata Tjuṯa.

Rubydock, whose brilliant red blooms cover the countryside after a heavy rain, is a plant native to western Asia and northern Africa. It is thought that it went wild from a garden in Alice Springs.

Living in the Desert

At Uluṟu, the Aṉangu work with the park rangers, sharing what they know of plants, animals, water holes, and all aspects of the land. Their knowledge of central Australia and its natural resources, and how to survive in its hot, arid climate, comes from generations of experience.

In the past, the Aṉangu moved often as they followed game and looked for food and water, constructing small shelters made from branches, leaves, grass, and other naturally available materials along the way. Today, in the more remote areas of Australia, some Aṉangu still lead a largely traditional life close to the land. At Uluṟu, about three hundred Aṉangu live in a small community called Muṯitjulu just north of the rock. Many of them work in the park. Like Aboriginal people in many other parts of Australia, they live in modern houses, drive cars, watch television, shop in

The cone-shaped flowers of the honey grevillea (kaliny-kalinypa) are prized for their sweet nectar. The flowers are either eaten, sucked, or soaked in water to make a sweet drink.

supermarkets, and enjoy the conveniences of today's world. They also retain some aspects of their traditional culture. This includes the hunting and gathering of wild foods, using both modern technology and traditional tools.

The Anangu are experts at knowing when and where to look for edible wild plants and animals. Plant foods that are part of the traditional Anangu diet include fruits, edible leaves, flowers, seeds, stems, and various roots, as well as edible galls found on certain trees. (Galls are growths produced by trees in response to invasions by insects.) Sweet foods that the Anangu eat include nectar from flowers, edible saps or gums from certain trees, honey ants (which have sacs of sweet fluid), and wild honey. Grubs, caterpillars, and insects are additional food sources. To obtain meat, fat, and eggs, they hunt kangaroos, lizards, snakes, birds, and other animals.

Desert plums (arnguli) ripen in March and April. They can be eaten raw or mashed and mixed with water to make a sweet drink.

Anangu collect seeds of wattle plants (tjuntala), then crush them and mix them with water to make an edible paste. Seeds are also sometimes ground into a flour.

TAKING CARE OF THE LAND

It is part of Tjukurpa that the Anangu are responsible for looking after the land. One of the ways they do this is through the use of fire. Burning the land encourages the regrowth of plants by clearing away old plants and returning nutrients to the soil in the ashes. The selective burning of small areas creates a patchwork of vegetation in various stages of growth. In this way there are always some places where food can be hunted and harvested, and other areas that will be ready in the future. The best time for controlled burning is in the winter, on cold, windless

days. Then, soon after the first spring rains, burned areas sprout with new life, providing nourishment for animals and people.

A park ranger watches carefully over a controlled burn.

Desert plants respond to fire in several ways. Many plants have fire-resistant seeds that will sprout after a fire. Other plants, such as spinifex, regrow from their root system, so that even after the top of the plant is gone, it can sprout from underground. When desert oak trees are burned, they are able to send out new shoots from their scorched trunks. Although mulga trees are killed by fire, their seeds need the heat of a fire to crack open in preparation for growth. Almost all the mulga trees that you see in Ulu<u>r</u>u-Kata Tju<u>t</u>a National Park today grew from seeds that sprouted in 1976 after a terrible fire destroyed more than three-quarters of the park's vegetation. The fire occurred at

The tiny leaves of the desert oak (kurka̲ra) grow on thin, delicate branches. The small leaves help prevent loss of moisture in the hot desert climate.

Seeds of the desert oak (kurka̲ra) are produced in large cones, which A̲nangu children sometimes play with as toys.

a time when burning had been prohibited for many years, which had resulted in a dangerous buildup of fuel. Patchwork burning has been practiced in the park since 1985, thus reducing the danger of wildfires burning out of control. Most wildfires occur in the summer and are usually started by lightning storms.

Australia's Red Center

Uluru-Kata Tjuta National Park is one of Australia's most popular tourist sites despite its remote location more than 1000 kilometers (620 miles) from most major cities. Every evening thousands of visitors gather at viewing spots to watch the slanting rays of the setting sun turn the nearly vertical walls of Uluru a fiery red. As the sun sinks below the western horizon, the rock changes gradually from orange to red to purple, finally becoming a black silhouette against the night sky. Visitors to the park can also walk the trails at the base of the rock, take guided walks with park rangers, and spend time at the cultural center, where exhibits and demonstrations tell about the Anangu. In all parts of the park that are open to the public, visitors are asked to respect it as the Anangu's home. Places that are particularly sacred or whose use is restricted to certain types of ceremonies are closed to visitors and photography is prohibited.

On the west side of Uluru a path leads to the top of

Uluru at sunset.

the rock. This is the traditional route taken by the ancestral Mala men when they first arrived at Uluru. The route of the climb is closely connected to Tjukurpa, and according to tradition, it is meant only for ceremonial use. The Anangu ask that visitors not climb Uluru, both because it goes against their spiritual beliefs and because the climb is dangerous. The Anangu suggest that instead of climbing Uluru, visitors walk around the base of the rock and take the time to experience the rock in its natural surroundings. The Anangu would like park visitors to view their world as they see it.

A PLACE OF UNIVERSAL IMPORTANCE

Uluru-Kata Tjuta National Park is one of fourteen sites in Australia that have been identified by the World Heritage committee of the United Nations as a place of universal importance. Once a place has been designated as a World Heritage Site, the committee helps to make sure it is maintained and protected for the benefit of present and future generations. Uluru-Kata Tjuta National Park was selected as a World Heritage Site for its outstanding natural features as well as for its lasting cultural values. It is a place of ongoing geological processes and of exceptional natural beauty. An excellent example of traditional human land use, it is directly associated with living traditions and beliefs of universal significance. There is no other site in the world like it.

People on the Mala walk are dwarfed by the high stone walls of Uluṟu.

Everyone who visits Uluṟu-Kata Tjuṯa National Park is amazed and inspired by the giant red rocks that rise above the desert floor. Visitors also have the chance to learn about the Aṉangu, whose rich culture has been tied to this landscape for countless generations.

GLOSSARY AND PRONUNCIATION GUIDE

(from the Pitjantjatjara and Yankunytjatjara dialects)

Anangu **[AH-nung-oo]** Pitjantjatjara word for Aboriginal people

aralapalpalpa **[AH-rull-ah-PAUL-paul-pah]** crested pigeon

arnguli **[ARN-goo-lee]** desert plum

Ikari **[EE-car- ee]** cave of the Willy Wagtail Woman

ili **[EE-lee]** desert fig

ilykuwara **[EE-lee-coo-wah-rah]** witchetty bush

itjaritjari **[EAT-jar-eat-jar-ee]** marsupial mole

kalaya **[KAH-lah-yah]** emu

kaliny-kalinypa **[CULL-in-CULL-in-pah]** honey grevillea plant

Kantju **[CARN-jaw]** gorge on northwest side of Uluru

kanyala **[CARN-yah-lah]** wallaroo

Kata Tjuta **[KAH-dah JAW-dah]** many heads; large rock
formation west of Uluru

kirkinpa **[KEER-kin-pah]** falcon or buzzard

kiti **[KEE-dee]** glue made from spinifex

kuniya **[COO-nee-ah]** python

kurkara **[CARE-kah-rah]** desert oak

liru **[LEER-roo]** poisonous snake

lungkata **[LOONG-gah-dah]** blue-tongued lizard

maku **[MAH-goo]** witchetty grub

mala **[MAH-la]** rufous hare wallaby

malu **[MAH-loo]** red kangaroo

Mutitjulu **[MOO-dee-joo-loo]** water hole at base of Uluru; also
name of Aboriginal community at Uluru

muur-muurpa **[MORE-more-pah]** bloodwood tree

nganngi **[NAN nee]** frog or toad

ngintaka **[NIN-dah-kah]** perentie lizard

Wallaroo (kanyala).

ngiyari [**NEE-yah-ree**] thorny devil lizard

ninu [**NEE-noo**] bilby

nyii-nyii [**NYEE-nyee**] zebra finch

paltu-paltupa [**PARL-too-parl-too-pah**] parrot pea

panpanpalala [**PAHN-pahn-pah-lah-lah**] crested bellbird

papa [**PAH-pah**] dingo

patupiri [**PAH-too-peer-ee**] bat

pila [**BILL-ah**] sand plains

pititjaku-pititjaku [**PEE-tee-jah-koo-PEE-tee-jah-koo**] butcherbird

Pitjantjatjara [**PIT-jan-jah-jarra**] dialect of the Western Desert language group

piyar-piyarpa [**PEE-yar-pee-yar-pah**] galah

puli [**BUL-ly**] rocky outcrop

puti [**BOO-tee**] flat, open woodlands

tali [**TAH-lee**] sand dunes

tarkawara [**TUCK-er-worra**] spinifex hopping mouse

tjanpi [**JARN-bee**] spinifex

tjantjalka [**JARN-jull-kah**] military dragon

tjilkamata [**JILL-gah-mah-dah**] echidna, or spiny anteater

tjintir-tjintirpa [**JIN-der-JIN-der-PA**] willy wagtail bird

Tjukurpa [**JOOK-oor-pah**] all encompassing view of the world and its creation

tjuntala [**JAWN-dullah**] wattle plant

Uluru [**OOL-oo-roo**] monolith also known as Ayers Rock

urtjanpa [**OR-jun-pah**] spearwood bush

walawuru [**WAH-lah-woo-roo**] wedgetail eagle

wanari [**ONE-ah-ree**] mulga tree

wayuta [**WHY-your-dah**] brushtail possum

Yankunytjatjara [**YAN-kun-jah-jarra**] dialect of the Western Desert language group

Butcherbird
(pititjaku-pititjaku).

INDEX

*Desert flowers bloom
after spring rains.*

Clumps of spinifex (tjanpi) and desert oaks (kurkara).

Author's Note

I would like to thank the media and information officers of Uluru-Kata Tjuta National Park and the members of the photographic subcommittee of the Uluru-Kata Tjuta Board of Management for their assistance on this project. I am grateful for the help of park staff during my visit and for information provided in "Park Notes" and other park publications, and for the recommendation of the following books: *Mingkiri: A Natural History of Uluru by the Mutitjulu Community*, compiled by Lynn Baker; *Uluru: Sharing Culture* and *Growing Up at Uluru* by Stanley Breeden; and *Uluru, Kata Tjuta and Watarrka*, a field guide by Anne Kerle. All of the photographs for this book were taken with a permit from Parks Australia and follow the required guidelines. In both photos and text every effort has been made to promote the cultural significance of Uluru and Kata Tjuta with respect to the wishes of the traditional Aboriginal owners.

Entrance to Mutitjulu water hole.